to dear Gusion

The Gentle Journey

A journey of spiritual discovery to inspire and encourage other fellow travellers

with heartfelt thanks
for all you have taught me
on the Metamorphic path

Blessings

Sylvia

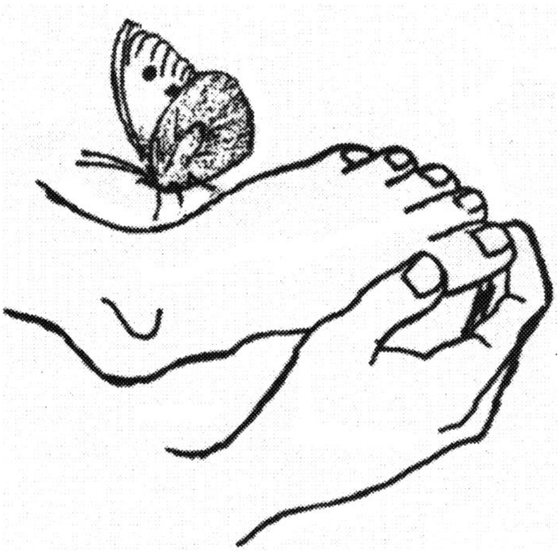

The Gentle Journey

By

Sylvia Briault

Date of Publication:
August 2002

Published by:
Simplicity Books
Casa Mia
Chemin du Moulin
St. Ouen, Jersey, C.I.
JE3 2FL
Tel. 01534 481257
Fax. 01534 483830

Printed by:
ProPrint
Riverside Cottage
Great North Road
Stibbington
Peterborough PE8 6LR

ISBN: 0-9543221-0-X

CONTENTS

Introduction

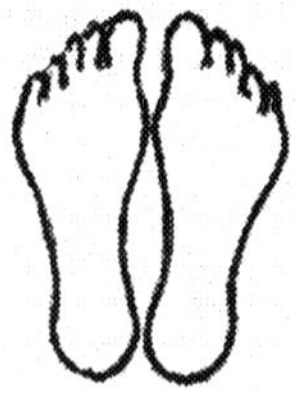

Dear Reader,

Welcome to my gentle journey.

Every single one of us, from the moment we are born until the moment we depart this earth, is on a journey - the journey of a lifetime.

It is only at certain times in our lives, mostly at crisis points, that we become aware of this. One major crisis occurred for me in 1986. Years of overwork, over-exerting myself, and burying emotions and deep issues resulted in major surgery and the discovery of an extremely rare, strange tumour known as pseudo myxoma peritonei (pmp for short).

Although I needed further major surgery twelve years later, I am able to say that the pmp became almost a friend because it has led me on a journey of discovery. A combination of my faith, the Metamorphic Technique and the pmp, has brought about many sequences of events, illuminating my journey and providing rich spiritual insights.

The simple book you now hold in your hands is the culmination of many experiences. I hope it will inspire and encourage you to value your own life journey and to perceive and appreciate the incredible gifts wrapped in the layers of everyday living.

Blessings,

Sylvia

Dedicated

to Robin, Duncan, Zoë, Jane and Oliver, my very precious and supportive family and to our late Titus, a unique and wonderful four-legged friend.

Also to two incredible, gentlemen, each a genius in their own particular way . . .

the late Robert St. John who discovered Metamorphosis, and Gaston Saint-Pierre who founded the Metamorphic Association.

Without these special ones I wouldn't be here now producing this book.

A deeper understanding of the Metamorphic Technique and of life itself

Apart from my faith, the Metamorphic Technique has helped me more than anything else during my journey. It has enabled me to face and deal with the buried emotions and issues of years gone by, gently and undramatically, one by one.

More than that, it has allowed me to dissolve the layers, patterns and masks of years of struggling and become my real true self! and release the potential that was trapped and on hold.

It has enriched my life beyond measure and given me the awareness to value each moment of each day and to appreciate the simple things in life.

It has helped me to find fulfilment and joy in life and to express my findings to others.

I can truly say that through the Metamorphic Technique, I have come to know and love myself (one of the most difficult missions in life!) and be happy and thankful that I am me!

The breath of life

The breath of life begins in gestation.
At precisely what point is beyond comprehension.
No-one has seen the spark being given.
No-one has seen the soul enter in.
Like all Divine gifts it is given in silence.
In simple complexity.
In wondrous simplicity.

All around us there's breathing,
unseen and un-noticed;
the birds and the insects,
the grass and the flowers are all breathing
the life-giving force.
Those wonderful trees so majestic and tall
are breathing in silence with rise and fall.

Unseen to our eyes. Unheard to our ears
the whole Universe is breathing and throbbing
with a beat and a pulse.

We're <u>all</u> a small part
of this incredible, incomprehensible
Breath of Life!

Metamorphic Touch

When you hold a seed you are holding an energy,
a divine spark of life – invisible power,
subtle power that will lead to new life,
new growing.

Now, in your hand it lies dormant, just waiting
for earth and water and sunlight.
Then comes the miracle, the signs of creating –
so simple, yet complex. So basic, yet mind blowing.

And so with our life force.
We are sometimes 'on hold'.
Like the seed we are waiting for certain conditions
to enable our opening, our blossoming – progressing.
Metamorphic Touch can be that trigger –
the gentle catalyst to release and allow
some deep-held emotion from distant gestation
to be brought into focus,
transformed and transmuted.

So gentle a touch – yet triggering so much
to take place within life.
It's as simple as breathing – as natural as being.

The Metamorphic Principle

How do you express those feelings so deep -
so enmeshed and disfigured, so fragmented and torn?
They rub without mercy like rough fingers on silk.
They catch and they snag in your heart and your mind.

So formless and wordless - yet always there,
like a wound slow to heal, like a recurring dream.
Is there, perhaps, in the depths of each one of us,
an element of autism, of terror and fear -
of inexplicable pain?
Is this how great symphonies come into being?
Is this how Van Gogh created his art?

These feelings are real - an energy manifesting -
silently shaping.
Once we acknowledge their existence,
their being-ness,
then the energy can move constructively.
So subtle a change. Yet life is fragility.
Gone in a second. New life in one act.

Acknowledge, accept, that the feelings are there,
however illusive or formless they seem.
Then - let them be!
That is sufficient for the transformation.
It's a Metamorphic Principle - the essence of life!

Simplicity. Complexity. Revelation and Miracle.

Song of Life and the Metamorphic Melody

There is a song of life
deep in your innermost being
that needs to be expressed.
Allow it space. Allow it freedom.
Allow it to move in creative fulfilment.

This song of life is a spark of light
waiting to be kindled.
Let it ignite. Let it a-flame.
Let it burnish in radiant dance

and then you become your song of life
giving voice to expression,
flowing with joy, moving with grace,
sharing with love in deepest contentment.

The Passing of Robert St. John

Such genius. Such insight. Such vision
encompassing more than the universe.
Such depth of knowledge
enhanced by experience
in searching and finding his own conclusions -
understanding life in all its complexity.

How sad the passing. Yet what a legacy
left to mankind - Metamorphosis!

A way of living life to the full,
of becoming who we are
and more than we would otherwise be.

Though his physical presence
is no longer here,
his Metamorphic Insight
has given humanity
a gentle, releasing

eternal touch . . . . .

Mosaic of Life

Each experience we encounter
on our journey through life
builds a mosaic of memory and energy.
Each feeling, each thought, each act,
each prayer, each song,
forms a colour and shape that fits in a space.

We are never aware, from moment to moment,
and day to day - even year to year,
of the patterns and pictures evolving together . . .
yet they form our being, the person we are,
and create around us a mosaic of aura.

We eventually realise as our earth journey ends
that a picture has formed
from the tiny pieces of mosaic events . . .
that from the dark and the light,
the bitter and the sweet,
the joyous and the sad,
a work of art and incredible beauty
has painstakingly been completed.

Life

I sit in the candlelight of a September morning
listening to the sound of the beating rain -
the first rains of Autumn.
The trees and shrubs in the cracked parched ground
are drinking in thirstily the falling droplets.

For me in the comfort and security of home
I can view the rain thankfully
watching it nurture and replenish the struggling plants
we have carefully tended.

Yet for others less fortunate or working outside -
their view of the rain will be different from mine.

And so with our lives . . .

We each view events from different perspectives -
and in the way that we think, in the way that we pray,
in the way that we eat our food,
in these everyday basics are incredible differences.

Each one is unique and complete
yet we all intertwine and relate
in the same living strands
of the one fragile web
of life and creation.

The Threads of Life

So many paths cross like silken threads
in the intricacies of life,
interweaving and blending
in harmonious brilliance.

In day to day living and sharing and meeting
with loved ones and friends and strangers unknown,
the threads keep on running
with rhythm and movement.

At times there are tangles and knots and distortions
and the threads sometimes break
causing heartache and pain,
but the threads are rejoined by the Master Weaver
with wisdom and tenderness
to ensure, in the end,
a complete masterpiece
with each thread in its place
creating perfection.

Lessons of Life

In youth we become impatient
with our elders who've lived so long.
We think we know far better than they.
We think their wisdom cannot apply.
Yet as maturity gently creeps upon us with the years,
we begin to see and understand
how wisdom evolves and grows.

And then we find we have much learning.
The lessons of life have taught us well.
We regret not having this special knowing
when we needed it most in the years before.

And then we find we are the elders
with young around us ignoring the help
that we so want to impart.
In the exuberance of youth they know better by far
and have to learn lessons as we did before.

And then we find we've gone beyond
the knowledge and the wisdom -
reverted to childhood simpleness in a strangely
unreal world.

And then we find we're ready to go
through the final door of our journey
to experience a whole new learning curve
leading to Eternity.

The Flowing River of Life

Life is like a flowing river - always moving,
ever onward, striving always to reach
the One Mighty Sea.

Sometimes there are rocks, boulders and debris
distorting and slowing the constant flow.

Sometimes there is flooding and spilling over,
speeding too fast with lack of control.

Sometimes there is dryness - a parched painful drought
with no movement or flow, when all seems to be lost.

Then there are times of beautiful ripples
gently flowing in sunlight with purpose and plan.

But in the fullness of time the river must reach
the Greater Expanse.
The end of the journeying -
the Ocean of Home.

Force of Life

There's a feel in the air of vibrations shifting,
a change in atmosphere, a different sensation.
We are gently slipping
away from Summer and into Autumn.

I felt this shift walking down by the sea.
Subtle nuance of tone as with colours and sounds,
barely detectable
yet sufficient to hone a different edge.

Memories surfaced as I walked in the dawn light,
of returning to school after the long vacation
and into the cool
of fresh mornings, dusky evenings.

I savoured the feeling deep down in my bones
despite a sadness for swallows departing
on journeys incredible.

They feel this shifting - this surging principle -
this primordial pulse
of the unfathomable,
indomitable,

Force of Life!

Living the moment is the only way
to be completely
alive

* * * * * * *

Seek not to understand all things.
Rather observe, accept
and appreciate.
With observation and appreciation
comes wisdom and understanding.

* * * * * * *

The secret of happiness
is to love life and live every day
accepting it as a cherished gift.

* * * * * * *

Flow with life's events
like a sapling in a storm
and you will remain unscathed.

* * * * * * *

The more we learn
the more we need to learn
how to apply what we learn
to our lives and way of living
before we teach others
what we have learnt.

* * * * * * *

Always observe. Never criticise.
Always accept. Never judge.
Always be open to the needs of others.
Always be aware of the very air
that you breathe
and give thanks for being alive.

* * * * * * *

When a loved one passes . . .

When a loved one passes how sad the loss;
how many regrets for things left unsaid.
How many memories flood into the mind
of the good times and bad -
the fun and the sadness.

The threads of life are strangely complex
and weave intricate patterns
of colours, shapes and specks.

When a loved one passes those threads remain.
Possessions and treasures may be shared
and divided;
some may be sold and some destroyed.
It's hard letting go but the more you release
the more you retain . . .
and the threads remain to weave again
a tapestry of life
in God's wonderful world.

Of Birth and Death

No words can describe the mystery of birth.
Such a natural thing. Such a wonderful thing.
Such a complex thing!

Then growth through the years
both physical and spiritual is taken for granted
without attention or contemplation.
But after the youth, the prime and maturity,
after the best years have passed. What then?

Then we consider what life is about.
Why we are here and where we will go.
What we have done and what might have been.
We collect much clutter along the way.
We accumulate, hoard and amass -
but then comes the time when we must depart
with nothing! just as we came!

No words can describe the mystery of death.
Such a natural thing. Such a wonderful thing.
Such a complex thing!

A greater appreciation of Nature

Ever since my childhood days I have had a love of nature. My early years were spent in a large busy town and we lived in a road one mile long full of square houses and tiny gardens.

I was absolutely enthralled when, one day, we had an owl staying in our tree at the bottom of our small garden. I can remember standing beneath the tree looking directly up at him and feeling a deep affinity.

During my gentle journey my love of Nature has grown and expanded and now I give thanks every day for being so fortunate as to live in our idyllic spot by the sea surrounded by trees and fields.

I hope my writings depict this deep affinity with Nature and that through them you will experience the closeness too.

The Flowering Cycle

For a flower there is first a bud;
this slowly opens and the flower blooms
in full beauty - but just for a while.

The petals fall, the colours fade
and the flower dies - but that is not the end!
There is a seed which falls into the earth.
In time it grows into a strong plant.
There is a bud. This slowly opens
and the flower blooms.

And so with us.
We are born. We grow. We blossom.
We mature - and then we slowly fade
until the silver cord breaks -
but that is not the end!

There is a soul - released -
which travels on to a higher plane
to be nurtured and learn.

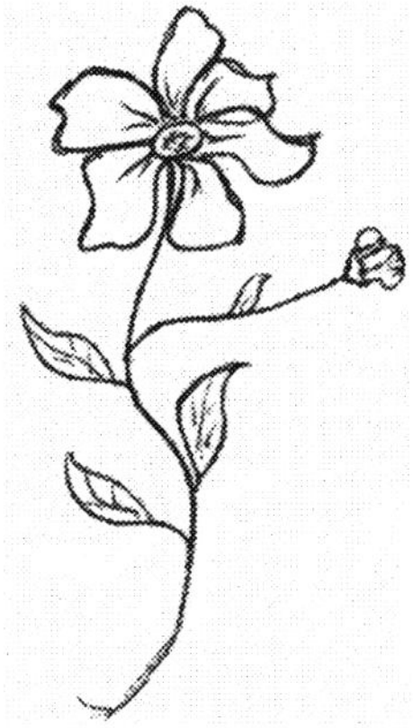

Then - there is a birth

and a child grows . . .

and blossoms . . .

and matures . . .

O dragonfly

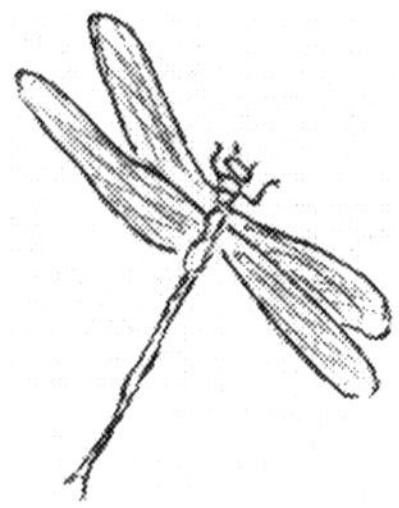

I feel so joyous when I see
the rainbow wings of a dragonfly
as it hovers and swoops so silently
shimmering in the sunlight gently by.
It seems to lift my spirits high
just watching its beauty and grace.
I try to capture it in my mind's eye to recall in a quiet place.

O dragonfly, your colours are rare . . .
not pink, not blue, nor aquamarine
but an exquisite blending of Nature's flare
with vibrant colours of every sheen.
I wish I could hold you in my hand
and keep your beauty by me
but that would be like preventing the sand from mingling
with
the sea.

All Nature's beauty comes and goes . . .
the sun, the moon, the seasons,
the flowers, the fruit and sudden rainbows
and for all of them are reasons.
Don't try to hold onto a moment of joy,
just savour it while it's there
and it will return for you to enjoy in pensive mood
or in quiet prayer.

Cat

She sits aloof with stare intent,
motionless, yet at ease.
She seems to have a strange content
and almost wears a smile.

Quite suddenly she tenses
and stretches out full length.
She uses all her senses
and grooms herself with care.

With velvet paws she moves with grace,
slips silently through the doorway . . .
out into the open space
on secret unknown journey.

Aloofness gone, she re-appears,
leaps on a lap, begins to purr.
The welcome lap she gently spears
with rhythmic paws stampeding.

Ode to the Swallow

Dear swallow of April
in freedom flight.
Harbinger of Summer
and warmth and light.
You bring joy to the heart
with your agile grace
and the way you chart
your journeys afar.

Dear swallow of April
I'm happy you're here
swooping and searching
far and near
over sea and shore
and garden and town
energising the air
with your presence and form.

Trees

A tee is much much more
than leaves and branches and sap;
it's a living breathing door
to Nature's endless tap
of energy and life.

It stretches upward to the sky
as if to reach its Maker;
yet it is anchored firmly by
strong roots so deep and safe
to weather storms and wind.

Trees cleanse the very air we breathe
making it pure and yet,
man fells them daily to receive
monetary gains and get
material wealth and more.

Trees give homes to creatures and birds
and food to living things;
they supply so much of our earthly need
how sad that man in his ugly greed
is burning them by the score.

Next time your hear the wind in the branches
singing melodies sad and clear,
give silent thanks amidst the breeze
for those incredibly, splendid, wonderful trees.

The Tree

I see the tree on my shopping trips
standing proud and tall - yet welcoming
with branches reaching far and wide.

I see the tree in all its aspects . . .
in winter bareness and silhouette beauty.
In new spring finery and full green leaf.

I see the tree in autumn gold
and fiery splendour.
I almost feel it greeting me
'though I pass at speed so fleetingly.

I look for the tree as I pass that way . . .
it's like a guardian protecting the home
where its roots go deep in silent strength.

I feel the tree and I are close -
some bond Divine melds us in spirit
and one day I shall walk that way
and embrace the tree I hold so dear.

The Dancing Leaf

A leaf danced across
my windscreen
playfully teased
by the strengthening wind.
It fluttered and turned,
leapt and somersaulted
in sprightly manoeuvres.

There was something of joy
and something of mischief
in the way that leaf danced
for timeless moments
engaging my attention.

Suddenly the wind increased its power
and the dancing leaf
was transported away
to perform wilder dances
travelling faster and faster.

That little leaf
that danced before me
told a story of changing times -
cooler mornings,
darker evenings,
balding trees and
Fire glow.

One dancing leaf for a few timeless moments
yet it coloured my day and touched my heart!

Drying leaves

There was a strange sense of movement
I saw in the leaves
lying strewn in their shapes of angles and lines
all along the way that we walked.
The strength of the wind
in its night time endeavours
had torn the leaves prematurely
and loosened their hold
so that now they lay lifeless,
flattened and dried
and yet -
this strange sense of movement
in the curve of the stalk
and the flow of their stance
in a motionless dance . . .

I felt it was saying
that death's not an ending -
but another formation in transmutation
to a level of being
that words can't describe.

Just some leaves lying drying
in artistic shapes - yet it spoke to my heart
in volumes of meaning that I cannot impart.
All I say in my ending is observe with your heart
and your mind and your being as well as your eyes
and you'll find life the richer
and a reason for living.

September Dawning

I sit in the dawning of a September morning
and hear the trilling of a bird singing
bringing freshness and newness -
a great encouraging and a needful confirming
that all things are working
and gently unfolding
to an unseen planning.

I feel a deep calming
pervading my being -
a sense of freeing
the sickening burdening
that was tightly engulfing
my onward progressing.

The candle flame's waning.
Daylight's expanding
and I feel a strengthening -
an upsurging and increasing
of vitality and coping.

Now from this dawning
and time of reflecting
I feel that I'm facing
the new day with welcoming.

In my heart there is singing.
In my soul there is hoping.
In my mind there is knowing
that all is flowing.

Ode to late Autumn

The change of season
is felt in the bones -
in the core of one's being -
deep and intense.

Sun is lower.
Night falls faster.
Leaves are dancing -
strip teasing the trees.

Crab apples fall
and roses grow weary.
Swallows long gone
and holly berries glowing.

There's a sense of longing
to be warm and cosy,
secure by the hearth
of one's own private space.

It's time for a dream world
of reverie and fancy,
time to reflect
and prepare for new growth.

The Eternal Cycle

The leaves of autumn are turning and falling,
fluttering and scurrying, crackling and rustling.
How do they know that their time has come?
What triggers their reaction and movement?
The mystery of Nature never reveals
the full wonder and scope
of her incredible depth.
Those leaves, now so dry, so brittle and lifeless
fall gently to the earth
to transform and transmute
to another substance - life-giving nutrients
to stimulate growth and replenish the soil.
So much losing and gaining,
renewing, re-using - Divine Conservation!

To our eyes the tree are now dead -
stark reminders of summertime gone,
dark winter to come.
Yet, unseen to our eyes
there is movement and growth
at some deep inner level
in those branches and trunks
a life-giving energy is silently working,
forming new shoots, new buds and new life.
As you watch the leaves turning and falling,
fluttering and scurrying,
think of the wisdom of the pulse
and the rhythm
of the eternal cycle
of life, death and re-birth.

Divine Conservation

The leaves of Autumn fluttering down
in a blending of hues from crimson to yellow,
burnt ochre to mellow
sing a story of thrifty creation.
The fresh beauty of spring,
glowing green with promise
has chameleoned into an artist's palette
of vibrant patterns and shapes.

A single leaf is a world of wonder.
See the silky skeleton of delicate lace
showing thread-like veins
of intricate formation.

Sense the frugal planning of transmutation
of the riotous colourings to earthful nutrition.

Watch the sleeping trees
standing silent and still
and hear with fresh ears
the internal growing,
the renewing, restructuring,
marvellous movement

of Divine Conservation.

Birds on the Wires

There must have been three hundred!
birds on the telephone wires
chattering softly together
neatly spaced out in lines.
From their lofty height
they could see far and wide
so some of them took off in flight
as they saw my approaching stride.

What do they talk about?
What do they say?
sitting so amicably
and slotting in place.

From time to time
they would fly in flocks
and feed from the seaweed
that was feeding the fields.
Then they would gather together again
fitting neatly along in rows
chattering incessantly their own refrain
or exchanging hot gossip - who knows?

There must have been three hundred!
birds on the telephone wires . . .

The Twilight Zone

At the close of day
as dusk is descending
is a turning point of stillness -
a timeless time
when the trees stand motionless
and the wind is silent
as though the world is adjusting
from the turmoil of day
to the solace of night.

The birds sing their songs
with a strangely sweet sadness -
a haunting farewell
to the day that is passed.

To sit in this time zone
in deep contemplation
is to savour the fragrance
of Nature's Grace.
From the twilight zone
with ease and skill
night falls so softly
enveloping all in a velvety darkness
of differing hue.
Only the moon in her changing aspects
silvers this velvet
with a moon glow shine.

The sap is rising

As you see the trees in their winter attire,
sombre colours and harsh jagged outline,
let your senses go deeper.
View more than the exterior
and listen intently - for THE SAP IS RISING!
The energy of life, unseen and unheard
is at work in the very depths
of those trees tall and stark.
A vital activity is taking place
in preparation for Easter's awakening.

If you see your life in a winter attire,
sombre colours and harsh jagged lines,
let your sense go deeper.
View more than the exterior
and listen intently - for THE SAP IS RISING!
The energy of life in answer to pleading
is at work in the depths of your own vital being.
A crucial movement is taking place
in preparation for your next awakening.

We see things only outwardly
in flashes, totally missing the nuances
and subtle indications.
If we let our senses go deeper.
View more than the exterior
and listen intently - we'll HEAR THE SAP RISING!
and the energy of life singing sweetly its song
as it works deep down in our bodies and souls
confirming a movement is taking place
in anticipation of our graduation.

Waiting . . .

I was waiting . . .
just waiting . . . for someone to come
and I sat on a stone in the fragrant shade
enjoying the sacred space.
My mind was free
of the burdens I'd left
and I sat and listened
to the sounds all around
as I watched the ants traversing the ground.
A tiny ladybird joined my space
and crawled on my paper
with her gentle grace.
Miniature spiders swung down beside me
on gossamer strands I could barely see.
A world of activity was silently moving
unaware of my presence but earnestly proving a
Greater Order
and Divine Control.

To sit and just be
in this timeless time . . .
living the movement – was completely sublime.

When my waiting ended
I felt refreshed and more able
to cope with the challenges
I knew lay ahead.

New Beginnings

In the hush of a dawn
when the earth is awakening
with birdsong and stirrings
and gentle light . . .
comes the birth of new beginnings.
It's like finding a new world -
a place unexplored!

When you rise in the dawning
and witness this birth
there's a renewal of spirit,
of heart and mind.
The doubtings and problems of yesterday
become fresh opportunities -
there is promise and excitement
in unfoldings unknown.

When problems surround
and you feel burdened and heavy,
try rising at dawn
and greeting the morning!

Give thanks for Creation
and beauty and sound . . .
then absorb and observe,

listen and receive!

Sun Down

As the sun sinks lower
in the western sky
a change of energy takes place,
invisible to the naked eye.
It's a special kind of grace.

As the sun drops lower
and the shadows fall,
there's a hush over Mother Earth.
The birds acknowledge
and softly call
and the wind smiles
in silent mirth.

As the sun disappears
and the twilight descends,
the night prepares
to slip gently in.
The energies move
as the day calmly ends,
and the night creatures' songs begin.

The Power of the Rain

See the rain.
Watch the rich cascades.
Feel the rain.
Receive the cleansing.
Hear the rain
and sense the rhythm.
Smell the rain
and see the growing.
Walk in the rain.
Let your cares wash away.
Splash in the rain
and be energised.
Accept the rain
bringing bounteous growth.
See it sparkling.
See it bouncing.
See it shining.
See it flowing.
See it glowing.
See the Power of the Rain . . .

Moonlight Reverie

O Moon shining bright for me tonight.
You shine so clear - seem almost near.
Just you and me, it feels that we
are alone in this place in our own private space.
Yet how many others, sisters and brothers
are looking tonight on your beauty bright
from places so distant - yet in this instant
we are one in deed in our innermost need
giving expression to an inner passion;
putting wordless emotions into fleeting notions.

O Moon shining bright for all tonight,
can you feel the tensions of a million sensations
wending your way? as many of us pray
to your Creator Spirit without limit?

Moon in your fullness and rhythmic wholeness
in the expanse of night a luminous sight
like a distant friend whose energies blend
into a way of giving hope for living.

O Moon shining bright all silvery white,
how many secrets and passions intimate
have been revealed in silent yield
while others sleep or a vigil keep?

O Moon so bright giving silent light
retain your mystery and distant history
for another millennium . . . ad infinitum . . .

A humble gratitude for home and family

When a serious health problem is suddenly revealed, it encourages you, after the initial shock, to re-evaluate your life and establish meaningful priorities.

This happened for me in 1986 when the 'pmp' was discovered and then in differing degrees at other times through the years.

An unexpected gift of a book on simple abundance prompted me to begin a Gratitude Journal. The idea is to write down at the end of each day, five things for which you can be thankful. They can be as basic as the roof over your head, your pet animal, or a wonderful rainbow, a glowing sunset, or simply a call from a friend.

Reading through the entries I had made caused me to realise the incredible richness in my life and the multitude of blessings I could count.

I hope that these humble writings will spark you to appreciate the immense richness in the everyday all around you.

Belonging

A feeling of belonging, of putting down roots.
A feeling of nurturing blossoming shoots,
of my being flowing with inner knowing
and the raw essence of self peeling layer by layer
to reveal the wealth of 'soul-full' living.

* * * * * * *

Casa Mia

I love this place in all its aspects.
I love the space of earth, sea and sky.

I love the sounds of the sea pounding near
and my wind chimes singing
and the birds calling clear.

I love the inside with space to breathe;
blue glass and sea glass, simple comfort and ease.

Yes, I love Casa Mia, my home by the sea,
with garden and nature, peace and serenity.

* * * * * * *

My Garden

My garden is a haven,
an oasis secure
where bees hum and drone
and the ants march in lines
of diligent order.

I can be free in my garden
to be myself -
comfy clothes, comfy shoes,
absorbed in my world
of clearing and weeding,
planting and tending in creative bliss.

My garden is a haven,
an island of peace
where birds build their nests
and the toads hide in pots
hopping silently by.

I can be free in my garden
to be alone -
alone with my thoughts
to contemplate and meditate
in the sweet fresh air,
both feet on the ground
yet my heart in Heaven.

My garden is a haven,
a sanctuary of delight -
an Eden of creativity.

My Bamboo Chimes

My bamboo chimes swing gently
in the wind of the morning,
greeting the new day with Nature's music.

My chimes have become almost a friend.
I'm aware of their presence
even when silent.
When no wind or breeze moves them to sound.

My bamboo chimes hang on the balcony
for passers by to enjoy
yet they're close to us inside.

Sometimes they chatter incessantly
when the wind is strong
and constantly changing direction and strength.
Sometimes they play softly tinkling a melody
as caressing breezes
playfully touch and then let go
and sometimes they clap like a thousand hands
when a fierce gale blows in from the roaring sea.

I hear them now in the December darkness
singing a song as a glimmer of dawn
heralds new day unfolding.

My bamboo chimes, once living plant,
live on in energy of sound and movement
free from season or sequence
to sing an eternal song . . .

My Blue Glass

One blue glass bowl from younger daughter
from Czechoslovakia
balanced in a back-pack.

One blue glass bowl from first daughter
with floating candles
and shiny pebbles.

One tall glass vase from only son.
Pure deep blue.
Long elegant shape.

One blue glass perfume bottle
from grateful client.
Circular shape and feminine.

Curly bottles and candle holders.
Little blue dolphins and tiny vases.
Bottles tall and bottles small.
All given with love and treasured dearly.
Not for materialism but for their beauty -
their elegance and grace
and the subtle energies they gently emit.

Yes I love my blue glass of deepest hue
and draw from its intensity with thankful heart.

Tea on the Balcony

Tea on the balcony.
Such a simple thing.
Such a blissful thing.

The soft March sun
gently warms my face
easing my being.

The wind chimes are singing,
the birds joyfully chirping.
There is drone of bee
and busyness of ant;
cherry blossom awakening
in the rays of the sun.

Tea on the balcony.
Such a simple thing.
Such a blissful thing.

Sipping the fragrance
of my golden tea,
my heart overflows
with childlike sincerity
in awe of creation
in its intricate detail.

'My cup runneth over'
sings a voice in my soul.
I'm at one with the world
and feel wonderfully whole.

The Little Rose Tree

I was given a gift - a heart chosen gift,
from a special friend,
for my caring in troublesome times.
The gift is a Rose Tree exquisitely formed
with silken roses shaped in a round.

To me it's far more than a silken Rose Tree -
it is Elegant Simplicity. Standing Tall.
Head held High. Perfect Composure.
Serene Supply!

After my own traumas sapping me dry,
it immediately lifts me each time I pass by.
In a prominent place to view constantly,
my posture improves almost instantly.

There's a grace and an elegance -
an inner blending of harmonious radiance
beyond comprehending.

Just a little Rose Tree fashioned in silk -
given with love -
yet for me it's a lesson
from the Divine Above.

Mordecai Toad

I found a toad,
a large dark green one
in a Garden Centre.
On impulse I bought him
and brought him home.
I gave him a name,
grand and Biblical -
Mordecai Toad.

It seems just right
and he sits outside
by the stable door
guarding and greeting
by the Welcome Stone.

I can just see his outline
as I approach the white gate
from my shopping trips
and he gives me a lift
and makes me smile.
He enjoys the sun
and weathers the wind.

I've been back several times
to look for another to keep him company
but he's happy alone.
He's unique and special
and I value his presence - my Mordecai Toad.

Morning Coffee

I grind the beans
and the aroma escapes.
In the cafetiere
the coffee releases its magical qualities.

In deep blue cups
our morning coffee
is a serious ritual,
sipped and savoured to the very last drop.

Coffee time is precious
and we plan our day.
I write my diary and record daily happenings.

We love morning coffee – it's part of our life.
I choose the beans carefully
with humble respect
and enjoy the whole process
with sincere gratitude.

Ode to Titus

Big brown eyes beseeching and wicked;
expressive sighs, grunts and lickings.
Such joy from the simplest things.
Walks in the lanes. A new toy bone.
His people coming home.

Such love and faithfulness. He's the same very day.
Such fun and zestfulness. He loves to play.

Our lives were changed the day he arrived,
re-arranged completely and how we thrived!
We couldn't be without him now.
He's completely won our hearts.

He sits on the stairs when people are leaving,
always the fourth stair, silently peeving.
He brings us gloves as we return,
and sometimes slippers so he can earn
a tasty reward.

Titus's coat is gleaming black, his proud bushy tail
held up in a curl.
He's strong and lithe, supple and sleek.
He travels fast when out on his walks.
He's agile and swift and never balks
from boldly defending.

He seems to know when we are low
and feeling out of sorts.
He sits beside us and offers a paw in canine empathy.

Oh, Titus! We could never be without you in our lives.
There was a time before you came -
but that was long ago.
Big black beauty with Biblical name.
You're firmly entrenched - we're glad that you came.

The Passing of Titus

When a faithful companion
of the four-legged kind
leaves this life as we know it for another plane,
how do you cope with the grief and the pain,
the sadness and loss? the intense desolation?

With no chance to say farewell or goodbye,
it's harder to bear and you have to cry.
The tears have to flow with no sense of pride.
It's important to show these feelings inside
and you can say it 'in spirit' -
he will feel it and know it.

There's far more to this life
than what we can see.
I believe in a Heaven with animals in it
and when our time comes to depart in spirit,
we'll be reunited in freedom and joy
for God in His wisdom created Eternity
so this life and the now is only a fraction
of the Overall Plan for humanity.

After he's gone

What a wise creator to give us tears
to release the pain that's trapped inside.
When no words can express
the loss and the emptiness
we feel at his going, the tears are so healing.

Coming home is the hardest with no greeting,
no wagging, no shaking, no licking!
Yet the morning is harder. There's an empty space
where his basket just fitted and how do we face
that incredible stillness?
He was so full of life with such vigour and grace.

Why? I keep asking did it have to be?
Did he take some pain that was meant for me?
As the days continue the hurt will decrease
and the pain subside but he'll always hold
such a special place deep down in our hearts
for he gave so much love . . .
he was sent from above.

His birthday

It's his birthday today.
He would have been nine!
It's so sad his life ended -
he was still in his prime.
He'd play games and chase rabbits,
he'd fetch slippers and get titbits.
He'd roll over and shake.
He would greet us and love us
when we'd been away
whether hours or minutes -
it was just his way.

It's so **empty** without him.
He was always just there!
He'd almost be smiling. He loved to be near.

Those days are now gone.
Only memories remain
and those we will treasure
forever and always . . .

Spencer

Spencer the bear
was a Mother's Day gift
selected with care and deep inspiration.
He's quickly become a part of our life
and we all succumb
to his special charms.

Spencer is cuddly
with wonderful eyes.
Every morning I huddle and hug him to bits.
He looks straight at you with a knowing look
as though he can follow
your thoughts and intentions.

Spencer sits in a special chair
with arms and rockers -
he's a fortunate bear surrounded by love.
He's so cuddly is Spencer and looks so real.
He's a wonderful sensor
of how we feel.

But he's really mine and I love him dearly
and we share special time
Spencer Bear and Me!

Sitting on the Balcony with Spencer

Sitting on the balcony on the wooden seat.
Spencer my bear beside me.
Together we're enjoying
the September sunshine -
a late summer bonus before Autumn rains.

Bird songs mingle with pigeons cooing
and large crows cawking.
There are distant jet 'planes
and cars and motor bikes
but here on the balcony it's peaceful and bright.

There are birds eating nuts and a robin trilling,
butterflies fluttering and bees busy droning.
There are spiders spinning and ants all scurrying.
White clouds are scudding
and leaves gently rustling.

Spencer and I are amazed to see
such a world of activity idly visible
from the wooden seat.

Sitting on the balcony with Spencer my bear
in glorious idleness and inner stillness

appreciating the vastness

of Mother Nature . . .

Inspiration from the Sun

I sat on the balcony in the afternoon sun,
in the easy chair, my chores all done.

I reclined on the chair and enjoyed the feel
of the sun and fresh air easing my being.

I let everything go . . . all worries and tensions
and entered the flow of living the moment.

The birds sang sweetly. I could hear the sea.
The leaves blew gently. There was drone of bee.

For a full half hour time stood still
in my personal bower of sacred dream.

Then from my reverie of pure meditation
came an energy of inspiration.

Free flowing concepts of creativity
brought colour and shape of wondrous intensity.

An idea was born, a formulation,
for a new art form in sound and motion.

Late afternoon Tea

I sip my Earl Grey tea
savouring the hint of bergamot.
In the late afternoon
the world has slowed down.
My wind chimes swing gently
in subtle melody
barely moved by the lazy wind.

In the distance an aeroplane
drones on high.
Inside, the clock sounds loud
in the silent room.

I love this time – the ending of day
and preparation for night.
It's a space for reflection,
to sit and savour the present moment.

Earl Grey tea in the late afternoon such elegant
simplicity.
Such blissful ritual.

Walking down by the Sea

This morning I walked down by the sea.
A new day had formed - vivid and vibrant,
promising and beckoning.
I walked by the water as the tide was turning
and the waves were churning
in rhythm and echoing along the shore.
The sun was rising and the air was fresh.
I felt the beat and the pulse
in tune with the Universe.
There was energy and vibration
and the world seemed new.

Just for these moments I was alone in time -
yet time meant nothing and couldn't be measured
in terms of freedom and joy.

I wanted to stay in this magical world
where time had no pressure and I was free!
But I had to return to the world of work
and commitments, duties and chores.
But I knew that another new morning would dawn
and find me again walking down by the sea . . .

Early morning low tide

I walked along by the sea today.
The tide was low and the rocks exposed.
There were rows of seaweed
across the wide beach
and hundreds of pebbles and stones.

Such a different feel
from the majesty of high tide
with its crashing waves and surf.
But there has to be high and low.
It's the rhythm of Nature . . .
the rise and the fall,
the full and the empty, the plenty and lean.

And so in life there are ups and downs,
sorrows and joys,
fulfilling times and frustrating times.

Yet it's only our attitude
to what befalls us
that makes it seem good or bad.

So enjoy the high tide - and also the low.

They bring balance and rhythm to life.

Late evening - St. Ouen's Bay

This evening I walked down to the sea
and entered a magical world.
The air was balmy from a day full of sun.
The crickets whirred
and the rabbits leapt high
their bobtails flashing white.
As I reached the shore
I could hear the sea
as the waves approached fullness of tide.
Faint wisps of pink tinged the western sky
and mirrored the image on shining water.

A gentle curve of a new young moon
showed proudly in the advancing dusk.
A late group of sand pipers
winged their way homeward
and I felt a deep sense of peace
and a closeness to God.

I felt a one-ness with all living things
and a sense of bonding
with others unknown
in far-away places all over the world
who were seeing that moon
and absorbing the beauty
of Nature and life's very essence.

I'm glad that I walked down to the sea
in the dusky glow of this magical eve.

The Essence of St. Ouen

We walked on the beach
in the expanse of the morning.

December. Deserted. Desolate.

A dreamscape of seascape;
jet black horizon and sinister clouds;
gulls painting pictures with flight in the sky.
Sea birds wistering ethereal sound.

The tide was far distant leaving the imprint
of its presence visible and freely available
to those who would seek and find the unique -
- the treasures so rare just waiting there.
Coloured glass glinting
and pottery chinting.
Driftwood rifting and seaweed shifting.

We walked on the beach
in the vastness of the morning.

Winter. Wildness. Wonderful.

A dreamscape of waterscape
constantly changing
second by second and cloud by cloud.

We walked on the beach
and savoured the feel
of St. Ouen in its Essence.

Stones

I love to walk along the beach
and see the stones, feel the stones,
hear the stones
chundling out of reach.

There are so many on the beach;
myriads of stones,
smooth and weathered stones,
rough and pebbly stones
tumbling out of reach.

I love to touch them on the beach,
my friends the stones;
sun-warmed stones, wet shiny stones
falling within my reach.

I love to walk along the beach
and see the stones, feel the stones,
hear the stones –
they've something special to teach.

Flowers from Alison

A special client brought flowers for me
in a beautiful bouquet.
There were orange and yellow chrysanthemums
and tall tiger lilies of burnished bronze.

I was already feeling the season changing
and it was like receiving
a taste of Autumn wrapped as a living gift.

Those flowers have really spoken to me
and brought me enjoyment
a hundred fold.

To give someone flowers
is to give living jewels
which nurture both body and soul.

Thank you, Alison, a hundred times
for your bounteous gift of pleasure.

For a friend's birthday

Finances didn't permit the purchase of a gift
to delight the eye and stimulate the mind
so instead I thought to give to you
some produce from the earth,
made with love and thankfulness
to add a taste of summer gone -
a hint of subtle sweetness, and then -
me thought, also, to pen a line
or two or three - or more -
to bring a smile and tax the brain
with nonsense - yet something of substance
on which to ponder and to contemplate.

Perhaps the Metamorphic Session
at such a timely hour
is even now producing different thoughts -
the faintest hint of a new approach
to the daily living and the distant goals
that shift their shape and structure
upon the far horizon.

The swing of the pendulum can go so far.

Can determine so much and open doors
to new understandings.

Yet, it's the delicate balance of the perfect poise
that allows us to be just who we are.

For Zoë my daughter at a turning point

So much potential,
So much life yet to live.
So much dreaming. So much yearning.
So much still to give.
So many pressures
looming and threatening.
So many choices, decisions, directions.

Equality. Duality. Complexity.
Where is normality?
Criticism. Cynicism. Mysticism.
Where is realism?
How to control the scales
moving and tipping?
How to restore balance
slipping and sliding.

Yet the searching yields finding.
The losing brings gaining.
Out of the chaos
serenity is born.
Out of the darkness
shines a new morn.

The mishaps of life
become signposts to wisdom.
The crises of life
open doors to freedom.

For my daughter Zoë at a vital time in her life

In the wide space of morning
take a breath . . . take a pause . . .
and survey all that's dawning
in newness of life.

See the world evolving in a blade of grass.
Hear Nature's solving in drone of bee.
Let desires of the heart
take root and grow
and begin to impart a serene intention
filled with zeal – yet composed to wait
for the time to reveal
the unique solution.

In the wide space of evening
take a breath . . . take a pause . . .
and release all that's grieving
in grateful surrender.

(Written during a stay at Southmoor Road, Oxford.)

For Zoë's friends in Oxford

I would like to have purchased a special gift
as thanks for my stay, and invading your space
but nothing seems right in your changing shift
so these words are written with warmth and grace.

I feel it an honour to stay in your home
so full of movement and changing scenes
yet sharing the simple basic tone
of life and living in all its seasons . . . so

thank you for sharing your special abode
and giving me time to spend with my daughter
and I wish you well in whatever mode
events unfold for you all in the future.

(Written at Southmoor Road, Oxford).

For Mother

So many things left unsaid.
So much we couldn't talk about.
You weren't able to share. I wasn't able to ask.
And yet we had happy times, fulfilling times
and peaceful times.

How sad that the years can pass
for a mother and daughter with no strong bond to unite.
Then comes the parting . . . the physical farewell.
Then comes the starting of more understanding.
With the physical parting comes a whole new dimension
of realisation.
The hurts are forgiven, the doubtings transformed.
On the wings of prayer we can reach Higher Planes
and put right the wrongs and fulfil the longings
of explanations.

For the physical parting is not an ending
but a new beginning of unlimited journeying
and Prayer is the Bond that unites the physical
with Heavenly Dimensions.
Just a longing of heart and sincerity of mind
when words will not form can achieve so much.

And so, Mother, this comes as a gift of intention
to say that I cared and still care and feel
though I couldn't show it, or express or define it
while you were here.

You gave me life and made me a home
and now I've become who I really am.

For a friend in pain

I feel for you, I really do.
So much to live for.
So many lessons painfully learnt
yet so many questions staying unanswered -
just beyond reach and not quite in sight.

I feel privileged to be sharing
some space and time
in your presence and aura
of acceptance and knowing.

The days are progressing.
The seasons turning.
Now lessons emerging and pain always surging . . .
yet there must be blessings
and gifts in the linings
of the black clouds rolling and the fate unfolding.

I cannot express all I truly feel
for words only access a limited field.
No words can describe the watching and sharing
unable to relieve the pain you are bearing.

No words can express the questions and searching,
the feelings and sadness - the momentous happening.

But perhaps these few phrases
fragmented and stilted, convey just a little
of my love and concern, admiration and wonder
at the way you are coping - and trusting and hoping
that all will be clear
when the time is near.

For my daughter Zoë on moving to her own place

Now in your new home,
settled, sorted and re-arranged,
take time to pause - to be - and really see
how far you have travelled
on your journey through life.

Take time to ponder, reflect and meditate
in a reverie of gratitude for all that has passed.
Then - be open to horizons new
opening before you, enticing you further,
enriching your knowledge
and expanding your trust.

Yet - seek always
simplicity of heart and the gentle way
so that in progressing ever onwards
you flow with the soul and nurture your being
for the soul at peace
and the heart full of joy
are priceless treasures beyond measure.

For my son Duncan on moving to his own place

You have travelled far
in your progress of soul-growing
and now, in your space,
close to earth, sea and sky,
new horizons will open
in expansion and promise.

You'll progress on your journey
of knowing self
and enjoy the process
as it unfolds and enriches
your day to day living.

I wish you Love.
I wish you Health,
Happiness and Joy
as you move to your home
and become who you are
with strength and purpose
to attain your potential
and fulfil your dreams.

A Fire in the Hearth

A fire in the hearth
brings another dimension
into your home.
You are never alone
with logs or coals
cheerfully burning.
There is movement and sound,
brightness and warmth
and constant activity -
flickers,
flames,
glowings and
sparks.
Ever moving.
Ever changing.
Mesmerising.
Energising.

You can stare in the flames
and let troubles melt.
As twilight deepens
there's a rosy glow
softening life and banishing woe.

Honour your fire
and tend it humbly.

Life is the richer
for a fire in the hearth.

Accepting the gifts and opportunities in all situations

Major surgery was a test for my Gratitude Journal, yet I managed to write in it almost every one of the days during that period.

Searching for the silver linings in the dark clouds of life and accepting with gratitude the opportunities in each situation as it unfolds, can bring untold rewards and become a way of living.

I hope you find encouragement in these personal experiences written from the heart.

Sojourn in Sark

The Anticipation

The time and location are booked.
The boat and finances arranged and completed.
Now comes the dream time of anticipation -
the waiting and the longing,
the planning and refining of preparation.

These weeks before sailing
to my special destination are a part of the process
of the whole intention to seek clarification
and confirmation of my true direction
along life's path.

Even now there are signs and some indications
of much in transition
in readiness for the true transformation
and manifestation!

Song of Sark

There's a song you can feel in your innermost bones
in this beautiful Island of Sark.
It's elusive and poignant, yet gently forming
as you wander the tracks and paths.
The melody sings in your soul and your mind
as you walk in rhythm with Nature's delight.

The open spaces and expanse of sea.
The simple life style and fresh clean air
sing their own special harmonies
blending together in one sensual, evocative
Song of Sark.

Sojourn in Sark

The Reality

Sark is a magical Island of beauty
with fields and hedges
and wonderful forests.
Sweeping landscape
and dramatic seascape.
Hidden beaches with lapping waves.

So much space and nature
and expanse of sea.
So many paths and tracks
to explore and wander completely free.

The life is simple,
direct and basic.
Living with nature yet delightfully classic.

There's friendship and caring,
kinship and sharing
yet space to be alone and free
to wander in joyful solitude.

The days in Sark seem longer.
Time is elastic and stretches forever.
The essence of moments is fuller and deeper
to be savoured much later
in darker days.

A sojourn in Sark both soothes and restores
body, mind and spirit
bringing refreshment and inner peace
in an oasis of retreat.

Stocks Hotel - Sark

Stocks is a place of olde worlde charm
and old fashioned courtesy -
a refreshing balm.
There's a special feel of bygone days
blending seamlessly with modern needs.

Delicious cuisine - out of this world
yet using organic veggies and herbs
lovingly grown in this magical isle.

Stocks is a place where you feel at home.
You feel welcome and nurtured,
pampered and cared for.
There's a wonderful ambience
and forgotten values
that makes Stocks unique -
a beautiful nuance that many seek.

In family ownership, run with care
Stocks offers a sojourn rare
where people return year after year
for that peace and caring
and timeless sharing.

Sojourn in Sark

The Return

Now home and into daily routine
but bombarded by horrors
of man's inhumanity -
the brutal terrors of bombing and destructing -
of thousands of lives wasted and lost.
A sickening jolt!

Yet from the ashes of mourning and losing
a world-wide empathy.
Caring and sharing and praying together.

So my own personal strategy
is on temporary hold
but the magic of Sark
and the timeless time
and the thoughts contrived there
will come to fruition
in due evolvement.

Already some strands
are taking firm hold
and gently and slowly with subtle sureness
my life will take shape
in a fresh open way
and boundaries will widen
and doors silently open.

The New York Terrorism

Depths of despair.
Empathy sharing.
Senses reeling.
Unbelieving.

Senseless deprivation.
Mindless motivation.
Miles of destruction
and ceaseless action.

The terror of terrorism.
Brutal barbarism
and shining heroism.
Entrapped escapism.

Yet out of the chaos
the sadness and losses,
a world wide unity of pathos
and caring,
a deep smouldering fire
to shine from the ashes
and burn through the dross
to lighten the way
for greater ethos
and values in living.

Before the operation

Calmness and composure
fought raging battles
with unformed fears and notions
of utter distortion.
Grotesque pictures
of shadowy shapes and monsters
floated ever changing before my eyes.

Slipping from real to unreal,
from fantasy to present moment
in constant upheaval.

Yet through it all a constancy of The One -
the only true Reality.
For the deep inner voice
would quell the clamourings,
mockings and lurkings
with the only answer there was -

Let go . . . and let God . . .

After the operation

Pipes and tubes and technology
singing soft chimes to alert the carers
to inject more fluid, more techno-science.
Trying to swallow on a monster pipe
ejecting surplus into a bag . . .
I had come through a battle to find another one raging.

Drifting into nightmares
of ugly distortions looming ever more huge
on a monster screen.
Constant pulses and pressures, checkings and testings,
joined to contraptions, I felt out of control -
whose was this body that I thought was me?

Kind voices, helping hands, lifting up,
pressing down, moving over, shifting sides.

Retching my heart out was the worst indignity . . .
water through straws to be forcefully discarded
and through it all hung the pang of pain like heavy metal.
But somehow it changed . . . like the turn of the tide
and fresh life and surgence brought healing relief
in rippling swathes.

Purple Anemone and Marble Vase
(both received as gifts in hospital)

Purple anemone
standing straight and tall,
proudly beautiful in natural grace.
You adorn so perfectly
marble vase, delicately formed
in intricate minuscule.

Anemone and vase
blend together as sentinel protection
softly guarding.
I feel your closeness,
your special presence heralding a sign
that wounds are healing.

So strong this feeling since flower and vase
came together in melding colours,
I take it to be a point of turning
for onward transforming.

A Hospital Space

So much space - so much time to think and be
yet not the environment
I would choose to reveal
the revelations surfacing free.

So many moments - so many hours
to reflect and conjecture
how the next phase will be spent.
A hospital bed starts investigations
into inner culture.
So much freedom - within constraints.
So much honesty - from within.
Dishevelled thoughts seem nicely honed
and distant notions finely tuned.

How to take these sculptured thoughts
back to the daily tide of living life
in all its ebb and flow?

There's a key I must take
to unlock the door of return.

For Robin

I see you now from my hospital bed
and wish that I could change
the years that were!
So many years we two have lived
together through life's pathways
in special bond of friendship and love
through many highs and lows.
Yet . . .
so much I with-held;
joys could have been richer
and sorrows more fully shared.

Why does it take the surgeon's knife
to bring about a change?
a new approach, a letting go
and allowing more to be?

So, home tomorrow
to be yet closer
and a richer way of living
life . . . in all its fullness.

I just need time and space
to weave the threads together
to form a masterpiece of art
in every intricate detail.

Spencer in Hospital

Spencer and I are in hospital.
I had the surgery. He's giving support.
He's had lots of cuddles
and been greatly admired.
He sits on my bed with his big brown eyes
concerned and caring.
We've just been watching
out of the window
at the wide grey sky and the cars passing by.

The days are long and the nights yet longer
but Spencer's nearness makes it easier.
The drip is down. The catheter gone
and I'm freer now and moving around.
Another day should see us returning
to Casa Mia by the sea.
Spencer and I are really close -
that special bond
between human and bear
that adds meaning to life
and a gift so rare.

Sleepless Night with Spencer

Spencer and I were awake really early.
We slept 'til four then were wide awake!
They made us some tea
and checked we were comfy -
such a very strange time to take a break!

Outside it was night -
intense and tight.
We longed for the bright
of the morning light.

And yet we thought and pondered and wrote
some lines of poetry to try and denote
how we felt and what was transforming
in these wakeful hours before the dawning.

We've made a plan for when we go home
to encompass the changes
that have gently grown
from our musings and ponderings,
reflections and wonderings.

So now we can't wait
for the moment they state
that Spencer and I are free to go home!

Beneath the Pain

Beneath the pain is a message real
with a particular refrain, unique and special
impelling us to deal with the situations
trapped beneath the pain.

If we look at the pain and hear the refrain
and confront head-on the locked constrains,
the knots will loosen
and the walls tumble down
and we'll see how small
was the first building block
that built the wall . . . beneath the pain.

Beneath the pain
is our soul's anguished cry
caught in the refrain of the pain's melody.
It's the only way for our souls to regain
attention and contact with our inner being.

Don't smother your pain –
look beyond and deep down.
Let your soul and your heart
direct your terrain.
You'll be surprised
at the treasures,
rich and rare,
you discover hidden
beneath the pain.

The ability to live in the present moment and a love of simplicity

Sometimes, just a few simple words can convey so much and transform our thinking or attitude.

During my journey, and through the Metamorphic sessions, a driving inner force has enabled me to shed much clutter along the way. It has brought great freedom and I have come to love and need simplicity and space in all aspects of my life.

Thus the extreme simplicity of the Japanese Haiku poem (only 17 syllables arranged in three lines) really appealed to me especially as it encourages us to live in, and appreciate, the present moment.

I do hope you will enjoy the frugality of words and subtlety of meaning in my simple Haiku writings and sense the bliss and contentment expressed in the sheer simplicity of the other writings.

Early morning air -
I smell the fresh crispness and
a season changing

* * * * * *

bats a-flittering
in the dusky summer air -
I see the world slow down

* * * * * *

Swallows gathering
confirming summer passing . . .
a tinge of sadness

* * * * * *

Distant voices float
on the sleepy summer air
I feel less lonely.

* * * * * *

Blue bottle buzzing
from window to window in
sleepy June sunshine

* * * * * *

Watching the ants move
I am mesmerised and learn
more about Nature

* * * * * *

Children's voices drift
over the expanse of sand
adding to my joy

* * * * * *

The sound of the sea
in my ears - I enjoy the
early morning walk

* * * * * *

Coffee beans grinding -
a wonderful aroma -
I savour each sip

* * * * * *

A cup of green tea
taken late in the evening
keeps me from sleeping

* * * * * *

Distant drone of 'plane
in the hot blue summer sky
makes me feel sleepy

* * * * * *

Damp misty sea-scape
hiding early summer sun -
dog walkers and me.

* * * * * *

In scented bubbles
I savour the silent warmth
in candle-lit bliss

* * * * * *

In the twilight hush
the gentle birdsong delights -
another day passed

* * * * * *

Moving flower pots
to sweep leaves in the courtyard
I find sleepy toad

* * * * * *

Mosquito buzzing
keeps me awake - in the morning
I find many bites

* * * * * *

My wind chimes moving
tinkling intermittently
making joyful sounds

* * * * * *

Unable to sleep
I hear the chimes of the clock
throughout the long night

* * * * * *

Oh caterpillar!
I see your potential yet
you eat my produce

* * * * * *

Sun dropping lower
over the shining water -
I prepare for winter

* * * * * *

Picking tomatoes
ripened by the summer sun
is a joyful task

* * * * * *

After the parchness
I enjoy the summer rain
soothing the dry earth

* * * * * *

Rainbow drops of dew
holding on to blades of grass
in the morning sun

* * * * * *

Bumble bee droning . . .
evocative feelings of
unending summer

* * * * * *

Sitting on the bench
in the gentle June sunshine
I forget worries

* * * * * *

Watching the children
in their uniforms playing
I feel a sadness

* * * * * *

The full moon shines bright
in the warm summer sky and
my bed stays empty

* * * * * *

The leaves of Autumn
write their poem in colours
of November sun

* * * * * *

The last shining leaves
cling tightly to the crown of
the silver birch tree

* * * * * *

Waiting for return
of my husband at lunch time
I enjoy my space

* * * * * *

I watch dragonfly
flashing rainbow colours in
the afternoon sun

* * * * * *

Walking on the beach
I savour the wide expanse
and sand in my toes

* * * * * *

Cutting lavender
to dry in bunches
gently soothes my soul

* * * * * *

Changing scenery
in Autumn gardens hinting
coming of winter

* * * * * *

Red streak of dawning
painting the new morning sky
in September light

* * * * * *

The size and structure of the human body
cannot reveal the nature of the soul within.

* * * * * *

Sunrise lights up the sky
with God's love.

* * * * * *

The shining stars
in the dark of night
communicate their silent poetry.

* * * * * *

Simple Abundancies

Simple abundancies today for me . . . my washing blowing
high and free in the sweet fresh air and energy.
Sipping my first outdoor cup of tea on the first day of spring
with the birds brightly trilling.

Little willow is bursting with catkins unfurling.
Potatoes are showing and onions are growing.
Buds are bursting and mats a-shaking in the first feel of
spring
since winter's long sleeping.
The energy's rising and spirits are lifting.
New buds are prising through tiny openings . . .

Simple abundancies! Sweet simple life!
nature's delicacies to combat strife.

(written on a 'cleaning the home day' in a break over a cup
of tea sitting outside in the little courtyard in the sunshine).

Soup

Simple soup
made from veggies and herbs
in a simple bowl -
yet fit for a king.

I love making soup
and all it entails.
Preparing and chopping.
Cutting and blending.
I love the colours
the shapes and textures,
the fragrance
of each special plant.

I give thanks
while I chop
and cut and cook
and seek a blessing
on all who have helped
in whatever part
to bring these ingredients
together for me.

In my soup - in my bowl
I have the fragrance of flavours
from many hands and many places.

Reverie at twilight

I sit in reverie
in blissful solitude
in the twilight hour
in pensive mood.

I wriggle my toes
and think fleeting notions
in sacred idleness
and soothing motions.

So rare these times
of contemplation . . .
just sitting and being
without justification.

The twilight has deepened
as my reverie lengthened
and I'm richly blessed
and greatly strengthened.

Just . . .

Just sitting savouring
the singing bird . . .

just watching the rainbows twirling
from the crystal prism
filtering sunlight . . .

just seeing the brightness
and absorbing the light . . .

just sitting and being
outside of time

is immensely healing
and wonderfully restoring.

I sit in a reverie of delight
living each precious moment
with delicious insight.

Just sitting and savouring
the singing bird . . .

just sitting and breathing
the September air . . .

just . . .

Look Well to this Day

The days flow by in quick succession.
Each one leaves its mark -
in a heart, in a losing, in a gaining,
in a trial, in a triumph,
in a line or a crease.
A day is but a fleeting part of a life span
and yet - one day makes history
never to be erased!

Savour this day.
Live every moment
in the full experience of the happening:
the bitter and the sweet,
the fast and the slow,
the joyful and the sad.

Live in the Now, not in the past,
nor wishing away the future.
Now is flexible, changeable.
You have the choice
to mould the events of today.
Make that decision. Write that letter.
Forgive that hurt. Send that invitation -
but do it Now!
When this day becomes yesterday
it is as though written in stone.

This day, then, is precious, unique.

It is all there is!

Purposeful Solitude

I was shattered and drained
and battered and delicate
so I took an hour -
an hour of purposeful solitude.
Beautiful space
without intrude
or word or presence
or human disturbance.
I sat in the arm chair
letting minutes tick by
in a dreamlike reverie
of exquisite peace.

A blackbird sang
in the afternoon rain
and my wind chimes
chattered a gentle tune.
The clock ticked a comforting
rhythm of time
and I absorbed these sounds
and lived the moments.

Just for this hour
there was only 'now'.

No worries, no chores,
no demands, no pressures - only blissful,
sacred, purposeful, solitude.

Synergy of the Sea

Such clarity of vision on this mid-June day.
Crystalline perfection of alluring horizon.
Vibrancy of colour and purity of air.
A magical experience to keep
in the tapestry of memory
to enlighten a winter's eve.

Across the ocean of deep velvet blue
shimmering sparklets of liquid gold
iridescently moving
in Divine interplay.

Synergy of the sea - sun energy on water!
creating a symphony of silent beauty
far beyond comprehension
or human design.

I felt humbled and privileged
to witness this miracle - liquid light and energy.
Colour and vibrance.

Synergy of the sea. Deep mystery and wonder.
Vastness of creation
and the wisdom of Creator.

(Written whilst sitting at La Rocque Beach, Jersey
on an idyllic June day. 11 June 2001)

An evolving sense of spirituality

Over the years and through my experiences, I have come to realise the importance of spirituality in my life. After all, we <u>are</u> body, mind and spirit and all three need to be nourished and balanced in order to live in a state of wellbeing.

Humanity, world wide, needs to see the Divine in all things everywhere - not just on Sundays and in religion.

I sincerely hope that my simple writings will illuminate your mind and ignite a flame to over-light your own spirituality.

If . . .

If you can see
the world
in a blade of grass;

if you can hear
a symphony
in the gentle breeze;

if you can allow
things to be . . .
and gently pass;

if you can find
the gifts
in life's difficulties;

then you will
live your life
with grace and ease

and touch
the essence of
Divine Soul Craft.

I saw a Dove

I saw a dove fly gently down to the stone bird bath in my garden. A moment later her companion flew down and together they drank their fill:

This tiny incident
warmed my heart
and brought upliftment.
Gave me a start
to a day that was dark.
I took the doves
to be a sign
that God's Love was guiding -
keeping me on line.

Sometimes we need
these little signs,
these sudden illuminations
so we are able to realign
and honour our imaginations.

I saw a dove
fly into the blue
with her mate above.
A handsome two
and my spirit soared
as they flew away.
I felt restored
and sailed into the day.

Pin pricks of Light deep in the Blue

Sometimes the darkness seems so intense
and our souls feel at total loss
as though we're hemmed in by an iron fence
with no room to think or to breathe.

And then comes a tiny glimmer of light
just a pin prick deep in the blue,
a ray of brightness like a Heavenly kite
lifting us up and giving us space.

A pin prick of light though so minuscule,
penetrates deep in the blueness and blackness
allowing more light to filter through
dispelling the gloom and foreboding.

So, I hope these words I have written here
will be pin pricks of light deep in the blue
to illuminate your way and open the sphere
of life fully and freely for you.

A shaft of light

A shaft of light
lit my darkness one day.
A tiny sunbeam
filtered through
a little crack in my darkened room
and bathed me in sunlight
with healing rays
and my heart opened wide . . .
let the light inside.

A shaft of light
took my darkness away.
That tiny sunbeam
was like a prayer,
a little miracle dispelling my gloom
filling me with sunlight
and Heavenly Grace
and my heart opened wide . . .
and let God inside.

A New Day - A New Way

A new day - a fresh beginning.
A new way - to start winning
instead of losing,
to try giving instead of taking,
to try praying instead of worrying.

A new day - unopened - unknown.
A new way - like a rose unblown
to try accepting instead of fighting,
searching for gifts, not complaining of loss.

Each day is a new day.
Each day is a new way.
That's why life is exciting
and challenging and thrilling,
but it has to begin with our own soul within.

No-one can live that new day for you.
No-one can start that new way for me.
<u>We</u> have to do it! absolutely commit.
Wholeheartedly, completely,
positively begin it!

and then comes the magic of transformation,
of self worth and self love -
a new aura of light
to shine from within
and glow from without.

Thank you, Lord

I'll sit a quiet moment more
'though chores and duties call me.
I'll sit and let your peace flow in . . .
listen for your voice.

I'll sit some moments in your presence
and feel your love surround me;
feel your strength surge through my body
bringing me fresh vitality.

Thank you Lord for being there
in all my moments everywhere.
Thank you Lord for blessing me now
when I felt weak and low.

I hear the singing of the birds
and see your bright sun shining,
yet it's in my heart and in my soul
that I really feel you living.

Thank you, Lord.

Blissful wonder

I sit in blissful wonder
at the newness of the day.
Rising early at dawning
is an incredible way
to experience the freshness,
the uniqueness of the living world.

The delicate songs
of the birds in their rapture
singing purely for joy
and just simply being
help me to capture
the spirit of Nature
in the paradox of complex simplicity.

Oh that I could stay
in this state of bliss sublime,
but life moves on
and is never still.
The activities of survival
increase in fervour
and I must enter this day
with purpose and will
but I know that The Author
of Nature's Wonder
is with me through good and ill.

Pondering on a Candle Flame

The flame of a candle
does more than give light -
it illuminates the soul
and symbolises that Greater Light.
It brings another dimension into life.
It brings comfort and hope in the dark of night.

To light a candle
for one in distress
is a caring action - like a prayer,
no matter where they are.

The flickering flame of a candle
demonstrates light, warmth
and movement
and the fragility of life.

For one breath
can extinguish the flame.
Only the touch of another light
can bring that candle flame to life again.

Yes - there is much to ponder
in the flame of a candle.

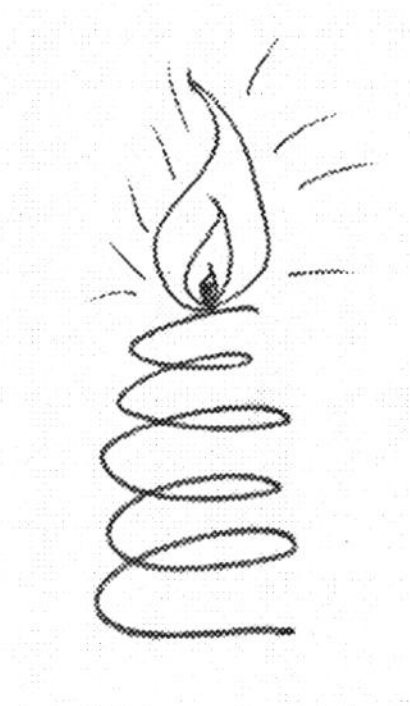

Thoughts

From small beginnings
momentous happenings.

The mighty oak
was once but an acorn!
Westminster Abbey
was first but a thought
in the Architect's mind.

Thoughts are of vital importance
because they manifest
in physical form.

Guard carefully your thoughts;

keep them noble,
keep them pure,
think lovingly,
think prayerfully,
think positively.
You will thus create Light
to shine through the Universe.

The Unseen Whole

To hold a dream gently.
To cherish its fruition
is to allow space and grace
and honour its creation.

To feel the deepest grief.
To have your heart torn - and break -
is to touch life in raw essence
and a character make.

To experience sheer joy
in the wonderment of life
is to see as a child
with a Heavenly sight.

To be truly at one
with the inner soul
is to come close to the knowing
of the Unseen Whole.

The Gentle Things

However sophisticated life may become
never lose touch with the simple things -
the meaningful gentle things of life -
the birth of a new morning,
the closing of day in the dusk of evening;
keep your mind open to the gentle things:
a dewdrop on a blade of grass,
a caressing breeze upon your face,
that frothy beauty of blossom in May,
the kindness of friends along the way.

Such things can't be measured
in money and prices,
they are there to be treasured amidst life's crises.

And if you would give your children a gift,
something precious and vital, long lasting, sustaining,
teach them the gift of appreciation,
show them the art of observation;
these lead to wisdom and understanding

and a love of life and a life full of love
with a tiny glimpse of Heaven above.

Music of the Soul

Music is a language
of unwritten words,
unexpressed emotions
and barely formed notions.
Music consoles
and touches souls.
Music reaches
far beyond
daily reality
into eternity.

Music calms
and brings a balm
beyond compare.

Music knows no boundaries
and cannot be contained . . .
it wells up in explodings
of expressions pained
and blissful joy.

Let the music of your soul
sing its story free
allowing you to reach your goal
and become
who you were meant to be.

Beyond the Sound

A wonderful silence
is to be found
beyond the sound.

After the talking has ended.
After the bells have tolled.
After the singer has sung the last note
there is a silence profound
beyond the sound.

A friend has a beautiful Tibetan bowl,
ancient and timeless
and given with love.
She struck it three times
with the special wood
and a magical resonance flowed.

For timeless moments
the bowl sang its song
then the last notes faded

and a silence so deep
and high and round
was found

beyond the sound.

Take this Moment

Take this moment . . .
as you read these lines
and savour its freshness -
its uniqueness.
It can never return.

Pause for a moment . . .
as you read these words
and feel your breath
work a hundred miracles
within your body.

Honour this moment
in the revelation of knowing
the stillness of time
that allows for renewing,
refreshing and healing.

Take this moment . . .
as you absorb the meaning
of being at ease
with one's self and life
and the Great Divine Light.

Take this moment

with Grace and Thanks.

The Power of the Paradox

Emptying our very selves
that we might be filled
to give again and go on giving;

seeing the chaos all around
yet feeling the peace
that passes understanding;

experiencing the depths of despair
yet brought through by miracles
from the releasing

this is the Power of the Paradox -
the mystery of life, death and rebirth.

Knowing the black clouds of sickness
yet finding the silver
in the linings of healing;

losing all that one owns
then directed a new way
with hope and receiving;

bearing the pain of personal loss
yet finding dimensions
of greater understanding

this is the Power of the Paradox
in life, death and rebirth.

Broken glass

Fragments and pieces - thousands of pieces -
shattered beyond repair.
Broken glass like broken dreams
smashed into sad despair

and yet

walk along the beach and see
the beauty of the coloured glass
now smooth and sleek and shining
midst the pebbles and the scree.
Touch the pieces glistening there
pounded and rounded by the power
of the mighty surging sea

and so

in life we have our broken glass.

Our dreams and schemes of daily living
shattered and scattered into disarray -
but all things gradually come to pass

and in the passing
sharp edges are gently smoothed
and beautiful mosaical pictures form
from the slivers and fragments
so battered and torn.

The Cocoon is open . . .

The cocoon is open and the movement of emergence
has begun in earnest.
This miracle move from one form to another
is sometimes painful, sometimes slow
yet each step is a part of the ongoing process
of reaching potential - continuing to grow . . .

If you watch another through this transition,
allow it to happen.
Allow the fruition of emergence and flight.
'Though well intentioned, your help would impede
the essential struggle for that one to succeed
on their unique individual special road
which no-one can know or direct or guide.

If the cocoon of your life is beginning to open
accept the struggle - refuse to be broken
or distracted or daunted
from the emergence of your own inner self,
beautifully poised to take your first breath
as the complete transformation of your own
brand new life.

(Inspired by the Sacred Path cards - from the North American Indians)

One Day

There's a phrase I have loved
since my childhood days -
it is simply 'One Day'!

In the stories of childhood
where a Princess slept for a hundred years,
there was suddenly 'One Day'
when the Prince came to change
the fate of that Princess
with one kiss or one touch delicately bestowed.

In our life times now
we may not have Princes coming to wake us
but after the long days of darkness and trial,
'One Day' there's a lifting - a changing -
new lighting - new hope.

Our problems may seem unending and bleak
with no sign of easing or moving or solving,
then suddenly - 'One Day' - out of the blue,
a complete transformation, a 'coming through'.

It has happened for me many times, many ways
so if you are having a troublesome year
that seems to be lasting forever and always,
take heart and take hope and rest assured
that 'One Day' very soon your 'Prince' will appear
to transform and resolve in miraculous ease.

Of Dreams and Visions

Nurture your dreams into fruition.
Cherish your visions towards completion.
So many a dream is lost in the hubble
of day to day living
and bursts like a bubble
scattered in ethers.

Hold your dreams gently close to your heart.
Write visions in ink - strength to impart.
All the great ones have needed a dream
and a vision rich -
an inner sunbeam
to carry them through.

Dreams have energy
and visions provide
nourishment for the spirit
to uplift and guide.

In the Fullness of Time

In the fullness of time is a wonderful phrase -
it has rhythm and shape and a timeless feel.
There's a great allowing
of expansion and space . . .
for natural movement
and evolvement to flow.

'In the fullness of time' allows all to transform
with an ease and a grace
of the universe spinning -
without seeming effort
yet Divinely precise.
There's a strange sense of comfort
in these simple words
'in the fullness of time'.

In the fullness of time trees blossom and flower,
fruit ripens and falls
and leaves change their colour
and release their hold.
In the fullness of time
the babe leaves the womb,
the child becomes an adult
and makes a new home.

In the fullness of time may you ponder these lines,
in pensive moments and times of reverie.
May they give you a sense
of all being right
with God's world and the Universe
knowing all will unfold in the fullness of time.

Love

At the height of loving, in the first intensity,
passion and appearance have much meaning
but in later years the sensitivity
of a deeper caring brings a greater loving
encompassing more than the physical.

Love cannot be critical, love must accept
the silvering of tresses
and a gentle softening
of contour and form.
For life through the years
brings both sorrow and joy,
times full of laughter
and times filled with tears.
There are times of much gaining
but hard times with losing.

As the sands of life
slowly accumulate
on the shores of experience
we have to prepare for the final wave
which completes our allotted span of time.

So allow love to become
the centre of all -
love for each other, our God and the world
for love really does
keep the Universe spinning.

The curve of a rainbow
is God's colourful smile
of Love and Promise

* * * * * *

The darkest night
always passes
with the glimmer of dawn

* * * * * *

In the stillness
you will hear
wisdom

* * * * * *

Special illuminations of The Gentle Journey

My gentle journey is still progressing and still unfolding but I felt an urgency to share it with others at this stage in the hope that it will inspire and encourage those finding their own personal life journeys difficult and unrewarding.

These special illuminations are still manifesting, even as I am putting these pages together, and there may well be a sequel to my Gentle Journey.

Oh that I could . . .

Oh that I could speak in a language of flowers . . .
in a language of flowing water and moonlight,
sunbeams and colour.
What wonderful writings and expressions
they would be!

Oh that I could write with the ink of my soul,
the tears from my eyes and the yearnings of my heart -
how meaningful my writings would be!

Yet on paper we can only write words
with the ink of a pen and the carbon of a pencil -
save were we to prick our fingers
and write in our life blood!

But with mindful imaginings we can access a level
that conveys these aspects . . . the deeper feelings
and raw emotions that lie unhealed and unbidden
beneath the surface of the exterior
we present to the world.

These words have begun a strange process for me
that I shall allow to unfold and blossom.
In fact, the process has transformed a pattern
and unveiled a key to unopened doors
of unexplored expression.

The patterns are changing and need time to settle -
like a kaleidoscope of youth,
shaken with hope and anticipation
for the new creation to be revealed.

(Written on Tuesday 5th March 2002 following a quiet time
and feeling a definite shift in levels of awareness.)

The Patterns have changed

The birdsong
has a greater clarity and sweetness;

the stillness of this new morning
a deeper poignancy

and the uncharted waters
of this new day unfolding
a more urgent calling for me.

The patterns have changed.
Time is of the essence
to be used more fully - yet joyfully,
mindfully - yet playfully,
prayerfully and contentedly.

New Timing

I feel I am in new timing now
where the order of tasks is unimportant
and achieving has less priority.

It is heart promptings
that take precedence now
and moving with the flow
of inner guidings.

A strange paradox is surfacing
where an urgency is dictating
a slowing-down of activity
thereby allowing the savouring
of the present moment.

Matters of importance are highlighted
through internal direction
and given attention in ease and grace
to complete and resolve
without tension.

An aura of blissful enchantment
has enveloped my being
and I feel blessed and enriched
beyond measure.

More than WORDS

Words have texture, shape and feel
as well as meaning and description.

Choose carefully your words -
they can be soft and gentle like silk and velvet
and caress the mind with beauty;

they can be full of zeal and vigour
like the zest of a lemon or an electric spark
and awaken and recharge the spirit;

they can be sharp and vicious like barbed wire
or broken glass and pierce and wound the very soul.

Words are our tools of communication,
our way of sharing one with another.
Words are a precious identification
of who we are and how we function.
The use of words is a delicate art
to be practised and refined
so that in the speaking, the very heart
of our intention is defined.

Ponder now the words you choose
lest, carelessly, in haste or turmoil,
you leash a torrent and infuse a bitter-sweet embroil.
Words once uttered have an energy
and cannot be un-spoken,
so be aware of synergy of thought and mind and token.

Then, when you speak you can be sure
that should your words return to you,
they'll be rewarding, strong and pure
embracing all things true.

My Healing Process

From trauma upon trauma many years ago
then layered and added
compounding the sorrow
I have now found a way to free my body
and its inner intelligence
to begin the process
of healing the hurts and senses.

From struggling and trying and working with formulas,
from analysing and probing
and sifting and loosening,
I have come to a place of simply allowing and being . . .
so child-like and beautiful.
A transparent innocence
of non-doing solace.

I've forgiven myself and others involved
in the pains and the wounds
inflicted in history
and I've given permission for the healing to start.
I've held back in the past,
somehow needing the pain
to make sense and explain in a martyr-like way.

But now it's so simple. With a firm intention
I can alter the structure
of the cells in my body.
It's the silence you see . . . making space and quiet
for the body, mind and spirit
to attune in harmony,
in ease and grace
in blissful Divine inner healing.